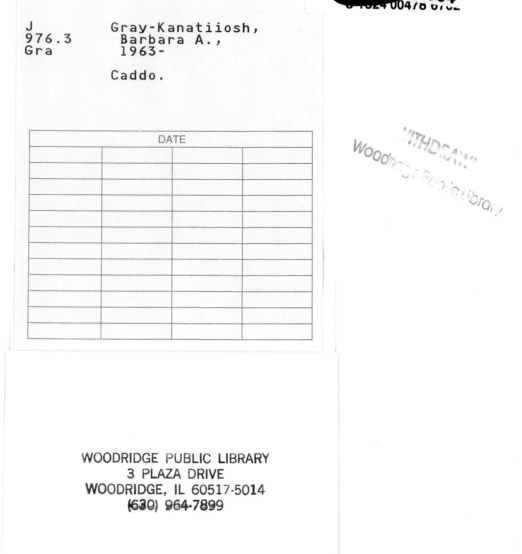

DATE			

Native Americans

Caddo

Barbara A. Gray-Kanatiiosh

ABDO Publishing Company

visit us at
www.abdopublishing.com

Cover Photo: © Pete Saloutos/Corbis
Interior Photos: AP/Wide World p. 30; Corbis pp. 4, 28, 29
Illustrations: David Kanietakeron Fadden pp. 7, 9, 11, 13, 15, 17, 19, 21, 23, 25, 27
Editors: Rochelle Baltzer, Megan M. Gunderson
Art Direction & Maps: Neil Klinepier

Library of Congress Cataloging-in-Publication Data

Gray-Kanatiiosh, Barbara A., 1963-
    Caddo / Barbara A. Gray-Kanatiiosh.
       p. cm. -- (Native Americans)
    Includes index.
    ISBN-10 1-59197-650-2
    ISBN-13 978-1-59197-650-9
    1. Caddo Indians--History--Juvenile literature. 2. Caddo Indians--Social life and customs--Juvenile literature. I. Title. II. Native Americans (Edina, Minn.)

E99.C12G73 2006
976.3004'9793--dc22
                                                                                    2005048319

About the Author: Barbara A. Gray-Kanatiiosh, JD

Barbara Gray-Kanatiiosh, JD, Ph.D. ABD, is an Akwesasne Mohawk. She resides at the Mohawk Nation and is of the Wolf Clan. She has a Juris Doctorate from Arizona State University, where she was one of the first recipients of ASU's special certificate in Indian Law. Barbara's Ph.D. is in Justice Studies at ASU. She is currently working on her dissertation, which concerns the impacts of environmental injustice on indigenous culture. Barbara works hard to educate children about Native Americans through her writing and Web site, where children may ask questions and receive a written response about the Haudenosaunee culture. The Web site is: www.peace4turtleisland.org

About the Illustrator: David Kanietakeron Fadden

David Kanietakeron Fadden is a member of the Akwesasne Mohawk Wolf Clan. His work has appeared in publications such as *Akwesasne Notes*, *Indian Time*, and the *Northeast Indian Quarterly*. Examples of his work have also appeared in various publications of the Six Nations Indian Museum in Onchiota, NY. His work has also appeared in "How the West Was Lost: Always the Enemy," produced by Gannett Production, which appeared on the Discovery Channel. David's work has been exhibited in Albany, NY; the Lake Placid Center for the Arts; Centre Strathearn in Montreal, Quebec; North Country Community College in Saranac Lake, NY; Paul Smith's College in Paul Smiths, NY; and at the Unison Arts & Learning Center in New Paltz, NY.

Contents

Where They Lived

Originally, the Caddo (KA-doh) were called *Kadohadacho*. This means "the real chiefs" in their language, which is part of the Caddoan language family. Later, the French shortened the name to Caddo. This name referred to about 20 tribes included in the Caddoan language family.

The Caddo homelands were located in the Southeast in the Red River valley. Their territory included present-day Louisiana and parts of Oklahoma, Texas, and Arkansas. Neighboring tribes included the Quapaw, Kiowa, Tunica, Natchez, and Osage.

A variety of landforms covered Caddo territory. There were rolling hills, rushing rivers, and

Caddo homelands were filled with beautiful bayous, where many different creatures lived.

lush forests. Forests contained magnolia, pine, oak, gum, ash, dogwood, walnut, and hickory trees. There were also swamplands and **bayous**.

Various types of ducks, geese, warblers, frogs, salamanders, and snakes lived in the bayous and rivers. Some snakes were poisonous such as water moccasins, rattlesnakes, and copperheads.

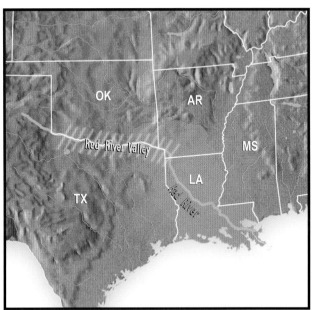

Caddo Homelands

Society

Caddo society was matrilineal. This means that a mother's **clan** name was passed on to her child. Clans were named after animals to provide a ranking among them. They included Beaver, Crow, Panther, and Wolf. Within each clan, religious and political leaders were most valued. These positions were inherited.

A high priest called a xinesi served all the villages. The xinesi was a spiritual guide for the Caddo. He conducted ceremonies, maintained the community temple, and performed religious services. There were also medicine men called connas. They performed **rituals** and cured sick people.

Each village had a chief called a caddi. This rank was passed from father to son. The caddi carried a polished stone staff as a symbol of his authority.

Every village also had a group of elders called canahas. The caddi consulted the canahas before he made an important decision. Then, the caddi had assistants called tammas carry out his orders. The tammas arranged hunts, made important announcements, and helped during ceremonies.

Each clan consisted of a main
village and other smaller villages.

Food

The Caddo were hunters, fishers, and gatherers. They were also expert gardeners. They grew corn, beans, squashes, pumpkins, gourds, melons, tobacco, and sunflowers.

Corn was an especially important crop. Many times it was the focus of ceremonies. Corn was used for both food and trade. The Caddo made breads, soups, and stews with corn. They mixed it with beans and meats to make the soups and stews.

The men hunted buffalo, deer, and bears with bows and arrows. They used traps to catch smaller animals such as rabbits, squirrels, ducks, and geese. They also fished for catfish, perch, bass, crappie, and sunfish. They used spears, hooks and lines, and handwoven nets to catch fish.

The women were responsible for gathering food. They collected wild onions, peaches, plums, and berries for their villages. They also gathered acorns, hickory nuts, walnuts, and pecans.

The Caddo ate many foods fresh. But, they also dried some foods to save for winter. To dry squashes, they cut them into long strips. Then, they wove the strips into a mat to dry in the sun. They smoked fish and other meats. And they mixed dried buffalo meat, **tallow**, and berries together to make pemmican. They ate pemmican during long trips.

Women crushed corn with wooden pestles and mortars.

9

Homes

Caddo villages were scattered near streams and rivers. Living close to water allowed the Caddo to leave quickly if hostile people approached their villages.

From a distance, Caddo homes looked like haystacks. These cone-shaped homes were built on high ground for protection from floods. And, the homes were usually arranged around earthen mounds. The mounds were used for religious and community events.

Caddo homes were about 15 feet (5 m) high. They were 20 to 50 feet (6 to 15 m) across the middle. To make a home, the Caddo bent narrow wooden poles. Then, they tied the poles together with strips of tree bark to form the frame. Next, they tied hooplike **sapling** poles onto the frame. These strengthened the frame.

Finally, the Caddo attached woven-grass mats to the frame. The mats overlapped like shingles on a modern house. This prevented rain from entering the home. Smoke escaped through the **thatched** walls.

Inside the homes, there were woven-grass storage bins attached to the walls. The Caddo slept on beds raised off the ground. They used animal hides and fur robes as bedcovers. And, they always had a fire burning in the center of the home for warmth and for cooking.

1 The frame was formed with wooden poles.

2 Sapling poles were tied onto the frame.

3 The frame was covered with woven mats.

Clothing

Caddo women made clothing from deer and elk hides. To do this, they scraped the remaining meat and hair from the hides. Then they **tanned** the hides. Finally they used **awls**, bone needles, and **sinew** thread to sew the tanned hides together.

The men wore **breechcloths**, fringed shirts, and leggings. The women wore woven-grass breechcloths under their dresses. During cold weather, both men and women wore robes for warmth.

The Caddo wore moccasins on their feet. These were made from buffalo hide because it was tough. Moccasins protected their feet from rocks and thorns.

Some Caddo **clans** removed their body hair completely, including their eyebrows. They used clamshells to pluck their facial hair. Some men pulled out all the hair on their heads except for a long strip down the center. This style is called a mohawk.

The Caddo also wore nose rings, earrings, and necklaces. These were made from shells, seed, and bones. Some Caddo wore a special oval-shaped shell necklace called a *gorget*.

Caddo clothing was
made from animal
hides. Mineral and
plant dyes colored
their clothing.

13

Crafts

The Caddo are known for their beautiful pottery. The women made plates, cups, pots, water containers, ornaments, and pipes. These pieces were precisely shaped and designed.

To make pottery, the women gathered clay from a riverbank. They kneaded this clay to make it workable. Then, they rolled it into snakelike lengths. Next, they stacked the clay to form a pot. They used water to smooth the inside and outside of the pot.

The women left the pot in the sun to dry. When it was dry, they used sticks to scratch lines and swirls into the pot. Then, they baked the pot in an open fire. Finally, they rubbed it with a polishing stone. The pot was then ready for use.

Sometimes, women made clay figures of animals and humans. They attached these figures to the pots to form handles. The women painted some pots to represent animals such as birds, frogs, and dogs. They made other pots with hollow walls. Then they placed pebbles inside to make rattles. The Caddo used rattles during some ceremonies.

Caddo women used
sticks to draw designs
on their pottery.

15

Family

The Caddo tended to marry between **clans**. When a Caddo man wished to marry, he gave the woman the finest gift he could manage. Her acceptance of the gift meant they were married.

Caddo villages contained **extended families**. Each person was expected to contribute to the survival of their village. They worked together to feed and protect each other.

The men prepared the fields for planting. They used digging tools made from bones or freshwater mussel shells. They also provided meat for their clans. Every year, the men went on a hunting trip in search of buffalo. They traveled for three to four months throughout eastern Oklahoma and the Texas plains.

While the men were gone, the women planted and tended the gardens. When the men returned, the women prepared the fresh meat. And, they used the new hides to make clothing.

Opposite page: Women used bone hoes to tend the crops.

Children

At birth, a Caddo infant was carried outside to meet the rising sun. The family prayed that the baby would have a healthy and good life. Then, they gave the newborn special gifts. A boy received bows and arrows to help him become a good hunter and protector. A girl received tools, such as **awls**. These would help her make beautiful clothing.

Children learned Caddo traditions by helping with chores and learning their responsibilities. Both boys and girls helped weed and plant the gardens. They also gathered nuts, berries, and plants.

Boys learned how to make tools and weapons by watching the men. Women taught girls how to make pottery, baskets, and clothing. Girls also learned the art of cooking. They were taught how to grind corn and nuts with a **pestle** and **mortar**.

But, children did more than just work. They had fun swimming and playing games. And, they had running contests. These activities kept them healthy. They also listened to the village elders, who told them stories about Caddo **culture**.

Caddo parents took their newborn outside at dawn. This was a sacred time.

Myths

Native Americans have many myths that teach them about life. The following Caddo story explains how the first people arrived in this world.

Long ago, all the animals and people lived underground. One day, an old man saw a dim ray of light. The light quickly came and left. He told the animals and people what he had seen.

After many days, the light returned. The Caddo decided to follow it. Soon, they found a cave. "I will see where the light comes from," the old man said. "I will take with me a pipe, fire, and a drum." He took these items for protection and guidance during his journey.

The man walked toward the light in the cave. Finally, he emerged into this world. He was standing between two rivers. Today, they are known as the Red River and the Mississippi River.

The man's wife followed, carrying corn and pumpkin seed. The people and animals were behind her. They all liked this world. Then a wolf emerged and sealed the opening with a big rock.

The people and animals began to cry because some of their friends were sealed underground. Today, the Caddo call this place *Cha'kani'na*, which means "place of crying." They continue to show respect to the first things that were brought into this world.

According to a Caddo legend, people and animals emerged from a cave into the world we live in.

21

War

The Caddo fought to protect their land and families. Prior to a war, several **rituals** took place. The warriors **fasted** to prepare their minds and bodies for battle.

A war dance was also held. At this time, the warriors danced around a fire. Then, they threw buffalo fat into it as a sacrifice. Finally, they rubbed smoke from the fire on their bodies. These rituals were believed to help keep the warriors safe.

The Caddo fought with bows and arrows. The bows were made of strong, bendable wood from Osage orange trees. And, the strings were made of **sinew**. The Caddo used glue made from buffalo hooves to attach feathers to the arrows. The feathers helped the arrows to fly straight. The arrowheads were made of stones or deer antlers.

During close combat, the Caddo used knives and clubs. These were made from stones, shells, or antlers. After the Caddo began trading with the Europeans, their weapons changed. Warriors started to use guns, hatchets, metal arrowheads, and iron knives.

When Caddo warriors succeeded in battle, the villagers gathered to celebrate. They watched the warriors return. Then everyone danced, and the warriors shared their stories.

For good luck during battle, Caddo warriors danced around a fire.

Contact with Europeans

In 1542, Spanish explorer Hernando de Soto met the Caddo along the Red River. The Caddo kept repeating their greeting *tejas,* which means "friends." So, Spanish authorities gave this name to the area. Later it was spelled "Texas."

Europeans did not return to Caddo territory for more than 100 years. Then, French explorer René-Robert Cavelier de La Salle encountered the Caddo. In 1682, La Salle claimed the Mississippi Valley for France. Soon after, the Caddo began trading with the French.

The Caddo had already established trade relations with their neighboring tribes. They traded bows and arrows and food for shells and other items.

The French traders wanted animal hides. So, the Caddo traded with other tribes to get these. The Caddo received horses and metal weapons from the Europeans in exchange for the hides. They also received copper kettles, glass beads, and premade clothing.

24

But, the Europeans also brought illnesses that were harmful to the Caddo. Many Caddo died from foreign diseases, such as smallpox. By the end of the 1700s, sickness had cut their population in half.

Trading was common among the Europeans and the Caddo. Each group had items that were valuable to the other.

White Bread

White Bread was a well-known Caddo tribal member. He was also a Ghost Dance leader. The Ghost Dance religion was brought to many tribes by the Paiute, another Native American tribe. The Caddo believed that it would renew their traditional lifestyle and make the new settlers leave. Then there would be no sickness, and the Caddo could live peacefully.

Around 1895, White Bread made a cedar pole that was to be used during Ghost Dance ceremonies. The pole was 12 feet (4 m) long and was painted black on one side and green on the other side. This represented death and renewal. The pole was said to have magical powers.

White Bread was a caddi from 1902 to 1913. During his time as chief, he traveled to Washington, D.C. There, he told the federal government about the difficulties that the Caddo faced. He fought to protect Caddo people, land, and traditions. White Bread died around 1922.

White Bread was a respected Caddo leader. However, his exact birth date is unknown.

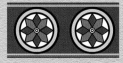

The Caddo Today

In 1803, France sold a large amount of land to the United States. This was called the Louisiana Purchase. It was the biggest land bargain in U.S. history. The land included Caddo territory. This was only the beginning of the Caddo struggle for land rights.

In 1830, the United States passed the Indian Removal Act. This forced eastern Native American tribes to relocate onto Caddo territory. Settlers also invaded Caddo land. The Caddo were being pushed out of their own villages. And, food was becoming scarce.

In 1835, the Caddo signed a treaty to sell their land. From this, the United States gained nearly 1 million acres (405,000 ha) of Caddo ancestral territory.

Today, the Caddo wear face paint on special occasions.

In 1938, three Caddo tribes became **federally recognized** as the Caddo Indian Tribe of Oklahoma. These individual tribes were the *Kadohadacho*, *Hasinai*, and *Natchitoches*.

Today, there are more than 4,000 Caddo. They work to protect their stories, traditions, and language. They attend many gatherings and ceremonies where they dance, sing, and celebrate their **culture**.

Caddo traditional dancers are ready to perform at a powwow.

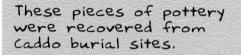
These pieces of pottery were recovered from Caddo burial sites.

This figure was carved by a Caddo person in the early 1800s. Human hair was attached to make it look more real.

Glossary

awl - a pointed tool for making small holes in materials such as leather or wood.

bayou - a shallow river.

breechcloth - a piece of hide or cloth, usually worn by men, that wraps between the legs and ties with a belt around the waist.

clan - an extended family related by a shared symbol.

culture - the customs, arts, and tools of a nation or people at a certain time.

extended family - a family that includes grandparents, uncles, aunts, and cousins in addition to a mother, father, and children.

fast - to go without food.

federal recognition - the U.S. government's recognition of a tribe as being an independent nation. The tribe is then eligible for special funding and for protection of its reservation lands.

mortar - a strong bowl or cup in which a material is pounded.

pestle - a club-shaped tool used to pound or crush a substance.

ritual - a form or order to a ceremony.

sapling - a young tree.

sinew - a band of tough fibers that joins a muscle to a bone.

tallow - the melted fat of cattle and sheep.

tan - to make a hide into leather by soaking it in a special liquid.

thatch - woven mats made of grass.

Web Sites

To learn more about the Caddo, visit ABDO Publishing Company on the World Wide Web at **www.abdopub.com**. Web sites about the Caddo are featured on our Book Links page. These links are routinely monitored and updated to provide the most current information available.

Index